Texas Jack's Famous Pralines Secret Recipe Book

DENNIS WALLER

Copyright © 2013 Dennis Waller

All rights reserved.

ISBN: 978-1482727401
ISBN-13: 1482727404

DEDICATION

This book is dedicated to a true aficionado of Pralines and honorary Chief of Texas Jack's Posse, Jason Williams of Duncan, Oklahoma. My thanks to you for your support and for bringing Aunt Bill's Brown Candy to Texas!

CONTENTS

	Acknowledgments	i
1	Texas Jack's Pralines	1
2	Praline Recipes	7
3	Cookie Recipes	31
4	Fudge Recipes	39
5	Aunt Bill's Brown Candy Recipe	49
6	Breakfast Pralines, Maple Bacon Pecan	51
7	Candied Pecan Recipe	53
8	A Little History about Texas Jack	57
9	About the Author	61

ACKNOWLEDGMENTS

I want to thank all the wonderful people that supported the Kickstarter Project for Texas Jack's Famous Pralines for making this a reality. And a special shout out to Pete Kelly, Jerry Stratton, and Oleg Medvedkov for their support!

CHAPTER ONE- TEXAS JACK'S PRALINES

The great thing about these praline recipes is you can change them around anyway you want. You can change out the pecans with whatever tickles your fancy. There are pine nuts, cashews, peanuts, hazelnuts, and many more. Same holds true with the flavoring. I encourage you to play around with it and try new things. If you are not a big fan of spice rum, then try out something different like "Wild Turkey American Honey" or "Kahlua" or even "Bailey's Irish Cream Whiskey" to try out some different flavors.

Remember there is no such thing as making a mistake in making pralines, only lessons learn. Well, I heard of one fellow using bacon and maple syrup in his pralines, sounds good doesn't it? So, don't be afraid to try out some new ideas.

Here are a few tips that should make your experience pleasant while making pralines. There are a few things you will need and without these, you are going to have a hard time being successful. Go, go on and read these tips, I say that it can't hurt.

The first thing you need is patience. Yep, you got to have some patience. Seems funny since the art of making pralines is being able to work fast once the mixture is ready to pour. So, if you run into a problem, just remember to have patience and learn from it and move on.

The second thing you need that is a "must have" is a Candy Thermometer. Without a candy thermometer, you might as well cook in the dark. I know some great chefs out there and no matter how good they are, they all use a candy thermometer in recipes that call for one. I betcha that even Richard Feynman, the Nobel Prize Winning Physicist would tell you the same thing, "Use it!" when it comes to a candy thermometer. Matter of fact, here is a photo of Richard telling you to use the candy thermometer, see?

The third thing you need is the right equipment. You need a good heavy saucepan, a two or three quart heavy saucepan is a good size. You want to have it deep enough to keep everything in the pot and not all over you and the stove. Trust me, this making praline business involves some hot temperatures so keeping in the pot is important.

In addition to a heavy saucepan, you'll need a big spoon for stirring. Get you a heavy duty metal or wooden spoon. Do not use a plastic spoon as it will become too soft with the temps that you'll be using. The best would be a wooden spoon as there is no heat transfer. I use a metal spoon with a rubber grip and like it just fine. It also serves as the right size for dropping the mixture into round pralines.

Along with an quality spoon for stirring get you a really good rubber spatula for helping in getting the mixture out of the pot if you are pouring your praline mixture into a slab. With a rubber spatula, you'll be able to control and help flow the mixture into a nice and even slab.

Another important thing to consider is using parchment paper, forget all about wax paper, when it comes to Texas Jack's Famous Pralines, parchment paper is the only way to go. Heck, Texas Jack uses nothing but parchment paper.

And lastly, when embarking on the journey of making pralines, have all of your ingredients ready to go. Once you get started, you are not going to have time running around the kitchen looking for that bottle of vanilla extract or measuring out the pecans. It's just too easy to have everything ready to go before you get started, so just do it.

Now, here are Two Most Important Tips that will make your experience a better one. Tip number one- When you are pouring out the mixture and want the end results to look like Gordon Ramsay made them himself, here is the trick. I use a pan made by Wilton. It is called the "Wilton Whoopie Pie Pan" and will hold 12 pralines, the openings are about 3 inches and make for the right size and the best part is, one of the recipes will fill up the pan, thus making 12 perfect pralines. You can get these at "Michaels" or any other nice shop that carries baking products, or just pick one up online. Now, I don't care what anyone tells you, take it from Texas Jack, use a "non-stick spray" on this here pan. If you don't believe me, try to get your pralines out of the pan without using a non-stick spray. Just trying to save you a headache here, so repeat after me, **"Use the Non-Stick Spray!"**

Second "Most Important Tip" - When you are pouring out the mixture and it starts to harden in the pot, just place the pot back on the stove with a few drops of water. Once the mixture is pliable, continue with the pour. You will find that any praline recipe using chocolate will want to set up rather quickly, so the trick is to reheat the mixture with a few drops to a quarter teaspoon of water when it gets too hard to pour. By doing this, you'll have the time needed to pour out the mixture in a clam manner that will benefit everyone within hearing distance of you, thus saving the need to use bad words towards me

Once you have your pralines made, they will keep for a few weeks but they won't last that long. I would suggest keeping them in a "air-tight" container to keep them fresh.

Remember to have fun and enjoy!

CHAPTER TWO- PRALINE RECIPES

Traditional Pecan Pralines

1 cup light brown sugar

1 cup granulated white sugar

1/4 cup water

1/4 cup evaporated milk

1 1/4 cups of lightly toasted pecans

3 tablespoons salted butter

2 teaspoons vanilla extract

Directions

In a heavy saucepan combine the white sugar, light brown sugar, water, and evaporated milk. Over medium to medium low heat stir mixture until the sugar is completely dissolved at around 200 degrees.

Bring it to a boil and cook until the candy thermometer reads 220 degrees, then add butter and pecans to mixture and continue to cook slowly until you reach 240 degrees.

Take saucepan off heat, stir in vanilla extract until well blended. Pour mixture on a parchment lined cookie sheet and spread out into a slab and allow to cool for about a hour. Cut into squares and enjoy! Or, if you prefer your pralines round, using a big spoon, drop a spoon full on the parchment paper until you have all the mixture used.

*To toast the pecans, place on a cookie sheet and place in a preheated oven at 350 degrees for 4 to 5 minutes. Remove from the cookie sheet and place in a bowl. I have found that by leaving the pecans on the heated cookie sheet, they will continue to toast. You may use the pecans as whole or chopped.

Chocolate Pecan Pralines

1 cup dark brown sugar

1 cup granulated white sugar

1/4 cup water

1/4 cup evaporated milk

2 ounces of Semi-Sweet Chocolate

1 1/4 cups of lightly toasted pecans

3 tablespoons salted butter

2 teaspoons vanilla extract

Directions

In a heavy saucepan combine the white sugar, dark brown sugar, water, and evaporated milk. Over medium to medium low heat stir mixture until the sugar is completely dissolved at around 200 degrees.

Bring it to a boil and cook until the candy thermometer reads 220 degrees, then add butter and pecans to mixture and continue to cook slowly until you reach 240 degrees.

Take saucepan off heat, stir in chocolate and vanilla extract until well blended. Pour mixture on a parchment lined cookie sheet and spread out into a slab and allow to cool for about a hour. Cut into squares and enjoy! Or, if you prefer your pralines

round, using a big spoon, drop a spoon full on the parchment paper until you have all the mixture used.

*You can use any type of chocolate you prefer. Some folks like using Baker's Semi-Sweet Baking Squares. The good thing about that is it comes in individually wrapped 1 ounce squares and it contains all nature 54% Cacao. Now, if you got the hankering for something fancy, you can substitute Baker's Chocolate with any Gourmet Chocolate like Godiva's fancy chocolate's.

*To toast the pecans, place on a cookie sheet and place in a preheated oven at 350 degrees for 4 to 5 minutes. Remove from the cookie sheet and place in a bowl. I have found that by leaving the pecans on the heated cookie sheet, they will continue to toast. You may use the pecans as whole or chopped.

Chocolate Coconut Pecan Pralines

1 cup dark brown sugar

1 cup granulated white sugar

1/4 cup water

1/4 cup evaporated milk

2 ounces of Semi-Sweet Chocolate

1 cup of lightly toasted pecans

1/2 cup Lightly Toasted Shredded Coconut

3 tablespoons salted butter

2 teaspoons vanilla extract

Directions

In a heavy saucepan combine the white sugar, dark brown sugar, water, and evaporated milk. Over medium to medium low heat stir mixture until the sugar is completely dissolved at around 200 degrees.

Bring it to a boil and cook until the candy thermometer reads 220 degrees, then add butter and pecans to mixture and continue to cook slowly until you reach 240 degrees.

Take saucepan off heat, stir in the coconut, chocolate and vanilla extract until well blended. Pour mixture on a parchment lined cookie sheet and spread out into a slab and allow to cool for about a hour. Cut into squares and enjoy! Or, if you prefer your pralines round, using a big spoon, drop a spoon full on the parchment paper until you have all the mixture used. Either way, you're going to have to move fast. If the mixture starts to set too quickly, add a few tablespoons of hot water and continue to stir till you're able to get the mixture used up.

*You can use any type of chocolate you prefer. Some folks like using Baker's Semi-Sweet Baking Squares. The good thing about that is it comes in individually wrapped 1 ounce squares and it contains all nature 54% Cacao. Now, if you got the hankering for something fancy, you can substitute Baker's Chocolate with any Gourmet Chocolate like Godiva's fancy chocolate's.

*To toast the pecans, place on a cookie sheet and place in a preheated oven at 350 degrees for 4 to 5 minutes. Remove from the cookie sheet and place in a bowl. I have found that by leaving the pecans on the heated cookie sheet, they will continue to toast. You may use the pecans as whole or chopped.

*Toast the coconut using the same method as toasting pecans but be careful not to over toast. You want to keep the coconut toasted to where it is still mainly white with a hint of light brown.

"Spiced Rum" Raisin Pecan Pralines

1 cup light brown sugar

1 cup granulated white sugar

1/4 cup water

1/4 cup evaporated milk

3/4 cup of lightly toasted pecans

1/2 cup raisins

3 tablespoons salted butter

4 tablespoons "Spiced Rum"

Directions

In a heavy saucepan combine the white sugar, light brown sugar, water, and evaporated milk. Over medium to medium low heat stir mixture until the sugar is completely dissolved at around 200 degrees.

Bring it to a boil and cook until the candy thermometer reads 220 degrees, then add butter and pecans to mixture and continue to cook slowly until you reach 240 degrees.

Take saucepan off heat, stir in the raisins and the spiced rum until well blended. Pour mixture on a parchment lined cookie sheet and spread out into a slab and allow to cool for about a hour. Cut into squares and enjoy! Or, if you prefer your pralines

round, using a big spoon, drop a spoon full on the parchment paper until you have all the mixture used.

*Our choice of spice rum is, " Crusoe Organic Spiced Rum" however you may use any spiced rum you like.

*To toast the pecans, place on a cookie sheet and place in a preheated oven at 350 degrees for 4 to 5 minutes. Remove from the cookie sheet and place in a bowl. I have found that by leaving the pecans on the heated cookie sheet, they will continue to toast. You may use the pecans as whole or chopped.

Chocolate Peanut Butter Pecan Pralines

1 cup light brown sugar

1 cup granulated white sugar

1/4 cup water

1/4 cup evaporated milk

3/4 cup of lightly toasted pecans

2 ounces of semi-sweet chocolate

3 tablespoons salted butter

4 tablespoons creamy peanut butter

Directions

In a heavy saucepan combine the white sugar, light brown sugar, water, and evaporated milk. Over medium to medium low heat stir mixture until the sugar is completely dissolved at around 200 degrees.

Bring it to a boil and cook until the candy thermometer reads 220 degrees, then add butter and pecans to mixture and continue to cook slowly until you reach 240 degrees.

Take saucepan off heat, stir in chocolate and peanut butter until well blended. Pour mixture on a parchment lined cookie sheet and spread out into a slab and allow to cool for about a hour. Cut into squares and enjoy! Or, if you prefer your pralines round, using a big spoon, drop a spoon full on the parchment paper until you have all the mixture used.

*You can use any type of chocolate you prefer. Some folks like using Baker's Semi-Sweet Baking Squares. The good thing about that is it comes in individually wrapped 1 ounce squares and it contains all nature 54% Cacao. Now, if you got the hankering for something fancy, you can substitute Baker's Chocolate with any Gourmet Chocolate like Godiva's fancy chocolate's.

*To toast the pecans, place on a cookie sheet and place in a preheated oven at 350 degrees for 4 to 5 minutes. Remove from the cookie sheet and place in a bowl. I have found that by leaving the pecans on the heated cookie sheet, they will continue to toast. You may use the pecans as whole or chopped.

Amaretto Pecan Pralines

1 cup dark brown sugar

1 cup granulated white sugar

1/4 cup water

1/4 cup evaporated milk

1 1/4 cup of lightly toasted pecans

3 tablespoons salted butter

4 tablespoons of Amaretto

Directions

In a heavy saucepan combine the white sugar, light brown sugar, water, and evaporated milk. Over medium to medium low heat stir mixture until the sugar is completely dissolved at around 200 degrees.

Bring it to a boil and cook until the candy thermometer reads 220 degrees, then add butter, and pecans to mixture and continue to cook slowly until you reach 240 degrees.

Take saucepan off heat, stir in the Amaretto until well blended. Pour mixture on a parchment lined cookie sheet and spread out into a slab and allow to cool for about a hour. Cut into squares and enjoy! Or, if you prefer your pralines round, using a big spoon, drop a spoon full on the parchment paper until you have all the mixture used.

*To toast the pecans, place on a cookie sheet and place in a preheated oven at 350 degrees for 4 to 5 minutes. Remove from the cookie sheet and place in a bowl. I have found that by leaving the pecans on the heated cookie sheet, they will continue to toast. You may use the pecans as whole or chopped.

"Bits of Brickle" Toffee Pecan Pralines

1 cup light brown sugar

1 cup granulated white sugar

1/4 cup water

1/4 cup evaporated milk

1 1/4 cup of lightly toasted pecans

3 tablespoons salted butter

1 teaspoon vanilla extract

4 ounces of "Heath English Toffee Bits"

Directions

In a heavy saucepan combine the light brown sugar, white sugar, water, and evaporated milk. Over medium to medium low heat stir mixture until the sugar is completely dissolved at around 200 degrees.

Bring it to a boil and cook until the candy thermometer reads 220 degrees, then add butter, and pecans to mixture and continue to cook slowly until you reach 240 degrees.

Take saucepan off heat, stir in the vanilla extract, and 4 ounces of the Heath English Toffee Bits until well blended. Pour mixture on a parchment lined cookie sheet and spread out into a slab and allow to cool for about a hour. Cut into squares and enjoy! Or, if you prefer your pralines round, using a big spoon, drop a spoon full on the parchment paper until you have all the mixture used.

*To toast the pecans, place on a cookie sheet and place in a preheated oven at 350 degrees for 4 to 5 minutes. Remove from the cookie sheet and place in a bowl. I have found that by leaving the pecans on the heated cookie sheet, they will continue to toast. You may use the pecans as whole or chopped.

Blue Agave Pecan Pralines

2/3 cup Agave Nectar

1 cup granulated white sugar

1/3 cup evaporated milk

1 1/4 cup of lightly toasted macadamia nuts or pecans

3 tablespoons salted butter

1 teaspoon vanilla extract

Directions

In a heavy saucepan combine the agave nectar, white sugar, and evaporated milk. Over medium to medium low heat stir mixture until the sugar is completely dissolved at around 200 degrees.

Bring it to a boil and cook until the candy thermometer reads 220 degrees, then add butter, and pecans to mixture and continue to cook slowly until you reach 240 degrees.

Take saucepan off heat, stir in the vanilla extract until well blended. Pour mixture on a parchment lined cookie sheet and spread out into a slab and allow to cool for about a hour. Cut into squares and enjoy! Or, if you prefer your pralines round, using a big spoon, drop a spoon full on the parchment paper until you have all the mixture used.

*To toast the pecans, place on a cookie sheet and place in a preheated oven at 350 degrees for 4 to 5 minutes. Remove from the cookie sheet and place in a bowl. I have found that by leaving the pecans on the heated cookie sheet, they will continue to toast. You may use the pecans as whole or chopped.

Mexican Chili Mocha Pecan Pralines

1 cup light brown sugar

1 cup granulated white sugar

1/4 cup water

1/4 cup evaporated milk

1 1/4 cup of lightly toasted pecans

2 ounces semi-sweet chocolate

1 1/2 tablespoons grinded coffee beans

1/2 teaspoon of cayenne pepper or to taste

3 tablespoons salted butter

1 teaspoon vanilla extract

Directions

In a heavy saucepan combine the white sugar, light brown sugar, water, and evaporated milk. Over medium to medium low heat stir mixture until the sugar is completely dissolved at around 200 degrees.

Bring it to a boil and cook until the candy thermometer reads 220 degrees, then add butter, pecans, cayenne pepper, and coffee to mixture and continue to cook slowly until you reach 240 degrees.

Take saucepan off heat, stir in the vanilla extract until well blended. Pour mixture on a parchment lined cookie sheet and spread out into a slab and allow to cool for about a hour. Cut into squares and enjoy! Or, if you prefer your pralines round, using a big spoon, drop a spoon full on the parchment paper until you have all the mixture used.

*You can use any type of chocolate you prefer. Some folks like using Baker's Semi-Sweet Baking Squares. The good thing about that is it comes in individually wrapped 1 ounce squares and it contains all nature 54% Cacao. Now, if you got the hankering for something fancy, you can substitute Baker's Chocolate with any Gourmet Chocolate like Godiva's fancy chocolate's.

*To toast the pecans, place on a cookie sheet and place in a preheated oven at 350 degrees for 4 to 5 minutes. Remove from the cookie sheet and place in a bowl. I have found that by leaving the pecans on the heated cookie sheet, they will continue to toast. You may use the pecans as whole or chopped.

Amaretto Almond Coconut Pralines

1 cup light brown sugar

1 cup granulated white sugar

1/4 cup water

1/4 cup evaporated milk

3/4 cup of lightly toasted almonds

1/2 cup of lightly toasted coconut

3 tablespoons salted butter

4 tablespoons Amaretto

Directions

In a heavy saucepan combine the white sugar, light brown sugar, water, and evaporated milk. Over medium to medium low heat stir mixture until the sugar is completely dissolved at around 200 degrees.

Bring it to a boil and cook until the candy thermometer reads 220 degrees, then add butter and almonds to mixture and continue to cook slowly until you reach 240 degrees.

Take saucepan off heat, stir in the Amaretto and the coconut until well blended. Pour mixture on a parchment lined cookie sheet and spread out into a slab and allow to cool for about a hour. Cut into squares and enjoy! Or, if you prefer your pralines

round, using a big spoon, drop a spoon full on the parchment paper until you have all the mixture used.

*To toast the almonds, place on a cookie sheet and place in a preheated oven at 350 degrees for 4 to 5 minutes. Remove from the cookie sheet and place in a bowl. I have found that by leaving the almonds on the heated cookie sheet, they will continue to toast. You may use the almonds as whole or chopped.

*Toast the coconut using the same method as toasting pecans but be careful not to over toast. You want to keep the coconut toasted to where it is still mainly white with a hint of light brown.

Crown Royal Maple Walnut Pralines

1 cup light brown sugar

1 cup granulated white sugar

1/4 cup water

1/4 cup evaporated milk

1 1/4 cup of lightly toasted walnuts

3 tablespoons salted butter

4 tablespoons Crown Royal Maple

Directions

In a heavy saucepan combine the white sugar, light brown sugar, water, and evaporated milk. Over medium to medium low heat stir mixture until the sugar is completely dissolved at around 200 degrees.

Bring it to a boil and cook until the candy thermometer reads 220 degrees, then add butter and walnuts to mixture and continue to cook slowly until you reach 240 degrees.

Take saucepan off heat, stir in the Crown Royal Maple until well blended. Pour mixture on a parchment lined cookie sheet and spread out into a slab and allow to cool for about a hour. Cut into squares and enjoy! Or, if you prefer your pralines round, using a big spoon, drop a spoon full on the parchment paper until you have all the mixture used.

*To toast the walnuts, place on a cookie sheet and place in a preheated oven at 350 degrees for 4 to 5 minutes. Remove from the cookie sheet and place in a bowl. I have found that by leaving the walnuts on the heated cookie sheet, they will continue to toast. You may use the walnuts as whole or chopped.

Macadamia Coconut Ginger Pralines

1 cup dark brown sugar

1 cup granulated white sugar

1/4 cup water

1/4 cup evaporated milk

3/4 cup of lightly toasted macadamia nuts

1/2 cup lightly toasted coconut

3 heaping tablespoons chopped crystallized ginger

3 tablespoons salted butter

1 teaspoon vanilla extract

Directions

In a heavy saucepan combine the white sugar, light brown sugar, water, and evaporated milk. Over medium to medium low heat stir mixture until the sugar is completely dissolved at around 200 degrees.

Bring it to a boil and cook until the candy thermometer reads 220 degrees, then add butter, macadamia nuts, and chopped crystallized ginger to mixture and continue to cook slowly until you reach 240 degrees.

Take saucepan off heat, stir in the vanilla extract and coconut until well blended. Pour mixture on a parchment lined cookie sheet and spread out into a slab and allow to cool for about a hour. Cut into squares and enjoy! Or, if you prefer your pralines round, using a big spoon, drop a spoon full on the parchment paper until you have all the mixture used.

*To toast the macadamia nuts, place on a cookie sheet and place in a preheated oven at 350 degrees for 4 to 5 minutes. Remove from the cookie sheet and place in a bowl. I have found that by leaving the macadamia nuts on the heated cookie sheet, they will continue to toast. You may use the macadamia nuts as whole or chopped.

*Toast the coconut using the same method as toasting pecans but be careful not to over toast. You want to keep the coconut toasted to where it is still mainly white with a hint of light brown.

CHAPTER THREE- COOKIE RECIPES

Here are four recipes for Texas Jack's Famous Cookies with the all-time favorites, Jimbo's Delight and Texas Jack's Calico Cookies. These recipes are easy to follow and easier to make. So enjoy!

"Jimbo's Delight" Pecan Walnut Chocolate Chip Cookies

1 cup butter- unsalted, (2 sticks) at room temperature

1 cup white sugar

1 cup light brown sugar

3 cups all-purpose flour

2 large eggs

2 teaspoons vanilla extract

1 teaspoon baking soda

2 teaspoons hot water

1/2 teaspoon salt

2 cups semi-sweet chocolate chips

3/4 cup chopped pecans

3/4 cup chopped walnuts

Directions

Preheat oven to 350 degrees

Combine the light brown sugar, white sugar, and butter and mix until smooth. Add eggs one at a time while beating mixture. Take the baking soda and dissolve it in the 2 teaspoons of hot water and add to mixture along with the 1/2 teaspoon of salt. When well mixed, add in flour and continue to mix. Add in chocolate chips, pecans, and walnuts and beat until well mixed.

Drop mixture using a large spoon unto an ungreased cookie sheet in 2 inch mounds about 2 inches apart. Place cookie sheet into the preheated oven and bake for about 10 minutes until the cookies are a nice crisp brown around the edges. Let cookies cool for about 5 minutes and remove to a baking rack and allow to cool off completely.

"Texas Jack's" Calico Butterscotch Chocolate Chip Cookies

You may substitute peanut butter chips in place of the butterscotch chips

Pecans are optional

1 cup butter- unsalted, (2 sticks) at room temperature
1 cup white sugar
1 cup light brown sugar
3 cups all-purpose flour
2 large eggs
2 teaspoons vanilla extract
1 teaspoon baking soda
2 teaspoons hot water
1/2 teaspoon salt
3/4 cup semi-sweet chocolate chips
3/4 cup white chocolate chips
3/4 cup butterscotch chips
3/4 cup chopped pecans (optional)

Directions

Preheat oven to 350 degrees

Combine the light brown sugar, white sugar, and butter and mix until smooth. Add eggs one at a time while beating mixture. Take the baking soda and dissolve it in the 2 teaspoons of hot water and add to mixture along with the 1/2 teaspoon of salt. When well mixed, add in flour and continue to mix. Add in semi-sweet chocolate chips, white chocolate chips, and butterscotch chips and beat until well mixed. At this time, if you desire, you can add the pecans, this is optional.

Drop mixture using a large spoon unto an ungreased cookie sheet in 2 inch mounds about 2 inches apart. Place cookie sheet into the preheated oven and bake for about 10 minutes until the cookies are a nice crisp brown around the edges. Let cookies cool for about 5 minutes and remove to a baking rack and allow to cool off completely.

Pecan Raisin Oatmeal Cookies

1 cup white sugar
1 cup dark brown sugar
1 cup butter, unsalted (2 sticks)
2 large eggs at room temperature
1 1/2 cups all-purpose flour
3 cups old-fashioned oatmeal
1 teaspoon baking powder
1 teaspoon ground cinnamon
1/2 teaspoon ground ginger
1/4 teaspoon cayenne pepper
1 teaspoon salt
2 teaspoons vanilla extract
1 teaspoon Spiced Rum or Rum extract (optional)
1 1/2 cups raisins or chopped dates
1 1/2 cups chopped lightly toasted pecans

Directions

Preheat the oven to 350 degrees

Beat butter, dark brown sugar, white sugar until light and fluffy in an electric mixer on medium-high speed. Turn mixer down to low and add the eggs one at a time then the vanilla extract.

In another bowl, combine the flour, baking powder, cinnamon, ginger, cayenne pepper, and salt together. Once the ingredients are well blended, add the mixture to the butter-sugar mixture in the electric mixer. When all ingredients are thoroughly mixed, add the pecans, raisins, and oats and beat until mixed.

Take the mixture and drop on a cookie sheet lined with parchment paper in 2 inch mounds about 2 inches apart, using the back of the spoon, slightly flatten. Place cookie sheet into the preheated oven and bake for about 12 to 15 minutes until the cookies are a nice crisp brown around the edges. Remove the cookies from the cookie sheet by lifting the parchment paper and move to a baking rack and allow to cool off completely.

Macadamia White Chocolate Chip Cookies

3/4 cup light brown sugar
1/2 cup white sugar
1 cup butter- unsalted (2 sticks)
2 large eggs at room temperature
3 tablespoons "Amaretto"
2 1/2 cups all-purpose flour
1 teaspoon baking soda
1/2 teaspoon salt
1 cup chopped macadamia nuts
1 cup white chocolate chips

Directions

Preheat oven to 350 degrees

In a large bowl combine light brown sugar, white sugar, and butter until smooth. Beat in the eggs one at a time then stir in Amaretto. In another bowl, combine flour, baking soda, and salt till well blended. Gradually add flour mixture to the butter-sugar mixture until well blended. Then add the macadamia nuts and white chocolate chips.

Drop mixture using a large spoon unto an ungreased cookie sheet in 2 inch mounds about 2 inches apart. Place cookie sheet into the preheated oven and bake for about 10 minutes until the cookies are a nice crisp brown around the edges. Let cookies cool for about 5 minutes and remove to a baking rack and allow to cool off completely or for about 30 minutes.

You may toast the macadamia nuts if you want to. Chop the nuts before toasting. Place in the preheated oven at 350 degrees for about 5 to 7 minutes, ensuring to keep an eye on the nuts as to prevent burning them.

CHAPTER FOUR- FUDGE RECIPES

With making fudge, please refer to the tips on making pralines as they hold true here too. Keep in mind that you can change up these recipes to fit the bill, so if you're not feeling like a nut, then feel free to leave them out. Or, try something different like using cashews instead of pecans. Experiment and make up some new recipes and make them your own, the key here is to have fun while making a great treat to share.

One thing about making fudge that is different from pralines is using foil paper in the pans when you pour out the fudge. With the foil paper lining, you'll be able to move the fudge with ease to the cutting board.

Like the pralines, the fudge will last a few weeks but it will not last once word gets out that you have a batch of Texas Jack's Famous Fudge made up and ready to eat. I do suggest keeping the fudge in an "air-tight" container and refrigerated to help keep it fresh. You can also freeze the fudge up to 3 months if you like.

Have fun and you'll be a Fudge Making Expert in no time!

"Texas Jack's" Famous Chocolate Pecan Fudge

3 cups white sugar

3/4 cup salted butter, (1 1/2 sticks)

5 ounces evaporated milk

7 ounces marshmallow cream

11 ounces semi-sweet chocolate

1 ounce "Nutella" spread (Texas Jack's secret ingredient)

1 teaspoon vanilla extract

1 cup chopped pecans

Directions

Line a pan or cookie sheet with foil paper. You may coat the foil paper with butter or with a nonstick cooking spray. For thicker fudge use a 8x8 inch pan.

In a heavy saucepan combine the sugar, butter, and milk and bring to a rolling boil while stirring constantly over medium heat. Continue to cook mixture for 4 to 5 minutes keeping the mixture below 238 degrees using a candy thermometer. After about 4 to 5 minutes, let the mixture get to 238 degrees then remove from heat.

Add the chocolate, Nutella spread, marshmallow cream, and vanilla extract. Stir vigorously until all ingredients are melted and well blended. Then add pecans and stir until well blended. Pour into pan and smooth into an even layer and allow to cool for 2 hours or to room temperature. Cut into squares and store in a air tight container. Does not require refrigeration but can be stored in the refrigerator or frozen.

Makes for a smooth, rich and creamy chocolate pecan fudge with a delightful hint of hazelnuts.

*You can use any type of chocolate you prefer. Some folks like using Baker's Semi-Sweet Baking Squares. The good thing about that is it comes in individually wrapped 1 ounce squares and it contains all nature 54% Cacao. Now, if you got the hankering for something fancy, you can substitute Baker's Chocolate with any Gourmet Chocolate like Godiva's fancy chocolate's. But remember that you are already using sugar so don't use sweet chocolates unless you like it really sweet.

Butterscotch Pecan Fudge

1 cup dark brown sugar

1/2 cup white sugar

1/2 cup butter- unsalted, (1 stick)

5 ounces evaporated milk

7 ounces marshmallow cream

1 bag or 11 ounces butterscotch chips

1 cup chopped pecans

Directions

Line a pan or cookie sheet with foil paper. You may coat the foil paper with butter or with a nonstick cooking spray. For thicker fudge use a 8x8 inch pan.

In a heavy saucepan combine the dark brown sugar, white sugar, butter, and milk and bring to a rolling boil while stirring constantly over medium heat. Continue to cook mixture for 4 to 5 minutes keeping the mixture below 238 degrees using a candy thermometer. After about 4 to 5 minutes, let the mixture get to 238 degrees then remove from heat.

Add the butterscotch chips, and marshmallow cream. Stir vigorously until all ingredients are melted and well blended. Then add pecans and stir until well blended. Pour into pan and smooth into an even layer and allow to cool for 2 hours or to room temperature. Cut into squares and store in a air tight container. Does not require refrigeration but can be stored in the refrigerator or frozen.

Pecan Caramel Fudge

1 cup dark brown sugar

1 cup white sugar

2/3 cup light cream

3 tablespoons butter- unsalted

1 teaspoon vanilla extract

3/4 cup chopped pecans

Directions

Line a pan or cookie sheet with foil paper. You may coat the foil paper with butter or with a nonstick cooking spray. For thicker fudge use a 8x8 inch pan.

In a heavy saucepan combine the dark brown sugar, white sugar, and milk and bring to a boil over medium heat then reduce heat to medium low while stirring constantly. Continue to cook mixture while maintaining a steady boil for 12 to 15 minutes keeping the mixture below 236 degrees using a candy thermometer. After about 12 to 15 minutes, let the mixture get to 236 degrees then mix in the butter and vanilla extract and remove from heat.

Let mixture cool down to 110 degrees, about 30 to 40 minutes. Beat mixture vigorously till fudge thickens then add pecans. Continue to beat fudge until it becomes thick and loses its gloss, usually about 8 to

10 minutes. Pour into pan and smooth into an even layer and allow to cool for 2 hours or to room temperature. Cut into squares and store in a air tight container. Does not require refrigeration but can be stored in the refrigerator or frozen.

Creamy Peanut Butter Pecan Fudge

1 1/2 cups light brown sugar

3/4 cup dark brown sugar

1/2 cup butter- unsalted (1 stick)

1/2 cup evaporated milk

1 teaspoon vanilla extract

3/4 cup creamy peanut butter at room temperature

1 cup chopped pecans

3 1/2 cups confectioner's sugar / powdered sugar

Directions

Line a pan or cookie sheet with foil paper. You may coat the foil paper with butter or with a nonstick cooking spray. For thicker fudge use a 8x8 inch pan.

In a heavy saucepan combine the dark and light brown sugar, butter, and milk and bring to a rolling boil while stirring constantly over medium heat. Continue to cook mixture for 4 to 5 minutes keeping the mixture below 238 degrees using a candy thermometer. After about 4 to 5 minutes, let the mixture get to 238 degrees then remove from heat.

Add peanut butter, vanilla extract, and confectioner's sugar. Stir vigorously until all ingredients are melted and well blended. Then add pecans and stir until well blended. Pour into pan and smooth into an even layer and allow to cool for 2 hours or to room temperature. Cut into squares and store in a air tight container. Does not require refrigeration but can be stored in the refrigerator or frozen.

CHAPTER FIVE- AUNT BILL'S BROWN CANDY

Aunt Bill's Brown Candy is from north of the border. Yep, it comes from all the way from Oklahoma but we are not going to hold that against it at all. Now this here recipe will provide you with a treat that will please anyone and will help introduce them to some real southern culture.

Aunt Bill's Brown Candy

Part A

1 cup white sugar

1/4 cup water

Part B

2 cups white sugar

1 cup heavy cream

1/4 teaspoon baking soda

6 tablespoons butter- unsalted, at room temperature

1 teaspoon vanilla extract

4 cups chopped pecans

Directions

Coat the inside of a 9x13 inch dish with butter.

In a heavy saucepan combine the 2 cups of white sugar and the 1 cup of heavy cream over low heat, stirring occasionally until the sugar dissolves. Set aside

In another heavy saucepan, bring "Part A," the 1 cup of white sugar and the 1/4 cup of water to a boil over medium-low heat until the sugar the dissolves. Increase heat to continue boiling without stirring until the syrup turns a deep amber. This should take about 8 minutes..

Take the syrup mixture and immediately pour into the heavy cream mixture, ensuring to go slowly with the pour while constantly stirring. (this process is best done by two people to ensure quality) Stir constantly over medium-low heat until the syrup mixture dissolves completely into the heavy cream mixture. Using a candy thermometer to ensure temperature control, increase the heat to medium. Stirring constantly, cook the mixture until the candy thermometer reaches 246 degrees, this should take about 10 to 12 minutes. Once reaching 246 degrees, remove from heat and add baking soda and butter and stir in till the butter is melted. Mixture will foam slightly but this is normal.

Let stand without stirring until the mixture cools off to 160 degrees, using the candy thermometer to monitor. This should take about 20 to 30 minutes. Once 160 degrees is reached, add and stir in the vanilla extract. Stir constantly until the candy begins to thicken and loses its gloss, this takes about 4 to 5 minutes.

At this time add the pecans and mix quickly as by now the candy is becoming stiff. Press the candy into the prepared dish and using your hands dipped in water, press the candy firmly into the pan and smooth out. Let candy cool completely for at least a hour till cool throughout. Cut into squares and serve!

CHAPTER SIX- BONUS RECIPE TEXAS JACK'S BREAKFAST PRALINES "MAPLE BACON PECAN PRALINES"

Texas Jack's Breakfast Pralines, "Maple Bacon Pecan Pralines"

1 cup dark brown sugar
1 cup white sugar
1/4 cup 100% Pure Maple Syrup
1/4 cup water
1/4 cup evaporated milk
1 cup lightly toasted pecans
1/4 finely chopped cooked bacon
3 tablespoons salted butter

Directions

In a heavy saucepan combine the white sugar, dark brown sugar, water, 100% pure maple syrup, and evaporated milk. Over medium to medium low heat stir mixture until the sugar is completely dissolved at around 200 degrees.

Bring it to a boil and cook until the candy thermometer reads 220 degrees, then add butter, bacon, and pecans to mixture and continue to cook slowly until you reach 240 degrees.

Take saucepan off heat and stir until mixture begins to thicken. Pour mixture on a parchment lined cookie sheet and spread out into a slab and allow to cool for about a hour. Cut into squares and enjoy! Or, if you prefer your pralines round, using a big spoon, drop a spoon full on the parchment paper until you have all the mixture used.

*To toast the pecans, place on a cookie sheet and place in a preheated oven at 350 degrees for 4 to 5 minutes. Remove from the cookie sheet and place in a bowl. I have found that by leaving the pecans on the heated cookie sheet, they will continue to toast. You may use the pecans as whole or chopped.

*Fry the bacon until completely cooked and crispy. Allow to cool and chop until you have a fine mixture. Set aside until you are ready for it. You can use hickory smoked bacon for added flavor or a bacon of your choosing. Applewood smoked bacon is another great choice too!

CHAPTER SEVEN- CANDIED PECANS RECIPE

Candied Sweet Pecans

Ingredients

1/4 cup light brown sugar
1/4 cup white sugar
1/4 teaspoon salt
1 teaspoon cinnamon
1/4 teaspoon ground ginger
1/4 teaspoon nutmeg
1 egg white from a large egg
1 teaspoon water
2 cups pecan halves

Directions

Preheat oven to 250 degrees

Take a cookie sheet and line with foil paper and apply a thin coating of butter or a non-stick spray and set aside.

In a bowl, mix the egg white with the water until well blended. Add the pecans and stir until the pecans are well coated with the egg mixture, remove and allow for the excess to drain from the pecans.

In another bowl, mix the light brown sugar, white sugar, salt, ginger, nutmeg, and cinnamon together until well blended. Add the egg coated pecans and toss until the pecans are well coated with the sugar mixture. Spread coated pecans on the foiled lined cookie sheet in an even manner. Place in the preheated oven and bake for one hour ensuring to stir every 15 minutes. Remove from oven and allow to cool completely to touch. Break apart if necessary and store in an air-tight container.

*You can take these candied pecans and finely chop them up and use as an ice cream topping.

Amaretto Candied Pecans

Ingredients

1/4 cup light brown sugar
4 ounces of Amaretto
1 tablespoon salted butter
1 cup toasted pecan halves
1 cup white sugar

Directions

In a small saucepan over medium heat combine the light brown sugar and Amaretto. Stir until the sugar is dissolved and add butter and toasted pecans. Continue to stir over medium heat until the mixture begins to caramelize. The mixture should be a dark amber color and thick. Do not rush cooking down the mixture but be mindful of not letting the mixture burn.

Remove from heat and pour out mixture on parchment paper and allow to cool. Once cool, break apart pecans and toss in a bag with the 1 cup of white sugar. Remove from bag, shake off any excess sugar and place in an air-tight container.

CHAPTER EIGHT- A LITTLE HISTORY ABOUT TEXAS JACK

Now Texas Jack Vermillion was a real live Gunslinger who rode with the Earp's in the "Vendetta Ride" just like in the movie. He was One Bad Hombre for sure and certainly was a friend to Doc Holliday.

John Wilson Vermillion, known as Texas Jack Vermillion (also known as Shoot-your-eye-out-Jack) was born 1842, Russell Co. Virginia. He was the second of 12 children born to William Vermillion and Nancy Owens. When the Civil War erupted in 1861, Texas Jack joined the Confederate cavalry under the command of General J.E.B. Stuart.

After the war Texas Jack married Margaret Horton on September 6, 1865 in Sullivan Co., Tennessee. The newlyweds moved to eastern Missouri where Jack accepted the position as Territorial Marshal for the eastern section of Missouri.

A daughter was born and named Mary and a second child followed. His name is unknown. Within a few weeks of the son's birth and while Jack was away from the home a diphtheria epidemic rambled across eastern Missouri killing Margaret and the children.

It has been written that grief stricken, Jack moved west. He surfaced in Dodge City, Kansas were he drank heavily, gambled frequently thus gaining a reputation as a " devil-may-care" gunslinger. It has also been written that when Dodge City burned for the first time that City Marshal and Deputy U.S. Marshal

Virgil Earp rounded-up 23 men he could trust to prevent lot jumpers. One of those men was Jack Vermillion.

Family history tells a story that Jack turned up in Montana and became involved in a saloon fight. Jack wasn't doing so well until someone stepped in to help. That someone was Doc Holliday. The legend continues that many years later Jack received a trunk shipped to him from Holliday.

As portrayed in the movie Tombstone, it has been written that Jack killed a man who accused him of cheating at cards. Unlike the movie, the gunfight was viewed as unfair and Jack became a wanted man. It was on the wanted poster that his name first appeared as "Texas Jack" Vermillion.

Texas Jack rode with Wyatt Earp during his vendetta ride and again was with Wyatt during the Dodge City War. He was considered a crack-shot with a gun by those who knew him.

Vermillion joined up with the Soapy Smith gang in 1888 or 1889, and was involved in the Pocatello, Idaho train depot shoot-out, in which a rival gang was trying to kill Soapy. He disappeared from known gang movements, but was reportedly involved in another gunfight in 1890.

In 1911 Jack passed away quietly in his sleep. It is rumored that his last meal was a praline.

*sourced
<http://captyak.tripod.com/texasjackvermillion/>

Here is another bit of history- "Texas Jack Vermillion did not accompany Virgil Earp as a member of the protective squad which escorted him to Tucson, March 20, 1882. Instead, Vermillion joined the vendetta posse March 21, 1882 in Tombstone, a day after the killing of Frank Stillwell in Tucson, thus Vermillion was not one of the 5 men indicted for Stilwell's killing. He presumably did participate in the killing of Florentino Cruz on March 22, and he had his horse shot out from under him during the fight at Iron Springs (March 24), in which "Curley Bill" Brocius was killed. Vermillion was himself not hit in that fight, but he had to be picked up by Doc Holliday after exposing himself to fire from the cowboys, while trying to retrieve the rifle wedged under his fallen horse."

*sourced - <http://en.wikipedia.org/wiki/Texas_Jack_Vermillion>

So, how did the name Texas Jack become part of this here praline recipe book? A few years back while making a batch of Pralines, the movie Tombstone was on TV. Someone asked what I called them and one of the folks sitting there on the couch said, "Hey! Name it after Texas Jack! Look, there he is!" And in an instant, the Pralines had a name.

With that, all I can say is, I'm sure glad we weren't watching Sponge Bob Square Pants!

ABOUT THE AUTHOR

Dennis Waller, author of several books, is recognized as an expert on spiritual experience, self-discovery, and exploring the human consciousness. As writer, speaker and philosopher, his teachings invoke an introspective view on how to discover one's true authentic self through a higher sense of consciousness and awareness. He teaches classes in the Dallas area on several subjects including Enochian Magic and Developing Your Psychic Abilities. He is best known for his work in the field of Indigos, people who possess unusual or supernatural abilities. His other fields of expertise include comparative religion, the law of attraction, and interpreting Eastern thought's relevancy to science and quantum physics. He is in demand as a guest speaker on radio programs, a lecturer at churches and life enrichment groups, and conducts workshops for Indigos.

He doesn't like long walks on the beach at night nor does he care for round balloons but does enjoy an occasional butterfly or cricket on a stick but only if served with fries. This bit of non-sense is included to see if you really read these bios. If you have then you will enjoy his sense of humor. Never take life too seriously, you will die someday so make the most of it, go out for an ice-cream, feed the ducks and tell someone you love that you do love them, even if you're mad at them, unless you're really mad like someone I know, then, maybe a phone call would be better.

Now, enough with the non-sense, but really, find a way to enjoy live and love!

Made in the USA
Columbia, SC
06 October 2017